Kids Edu Caring Place

Happy Animals Everywhere In English & Temne

By: Kenyatta Smith-Simpson & Kendrick Simpson

Kids Edu Caring Place
Happy Animals Everywhere in Temne & English

Written & Published By: Kenyatta Smith-Simpson & Kendrick Simpson

For Information contact KECP Childrens Books.
700 Springfield Avenue Baltimore, Maryland 21212

www.KidsEduCaringPlace.com
ISBN:979-8-9860978-2-4
Book Designed By: Kenyatta Smith-Simpson

This book belongs to a
Kidscredible kid named:

____

Happy Animals Everywhere

Goat - Def
The goat is chewing on the grass.

Snail - Antikol

The snail is sitting on a log.

Cat - Ayaree

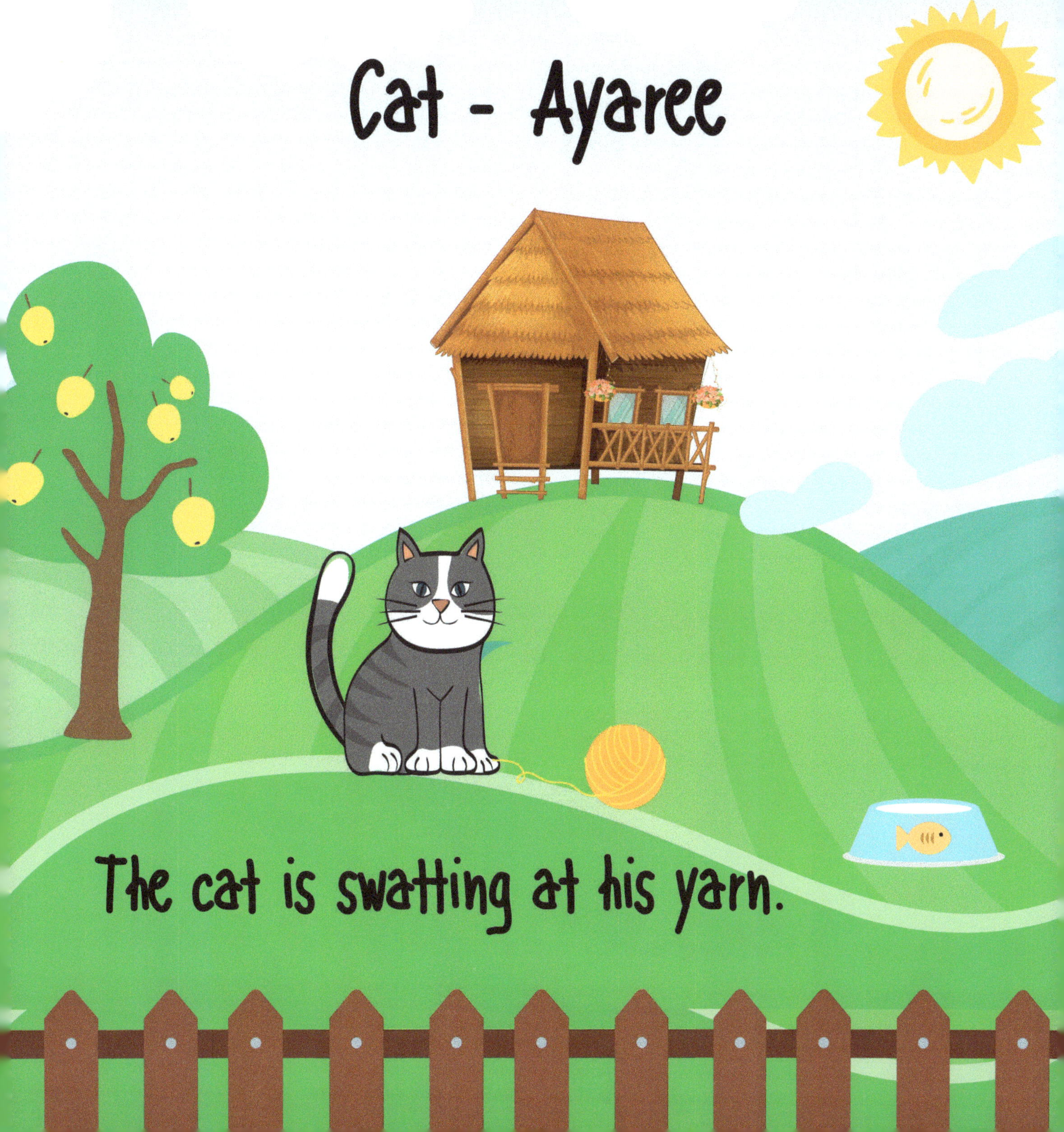

The cat is swatting at his yarn.

Hen - Kabet

The hen is walking around the yard.

Snake - Umbook
The snake is slithering past the sticks.

Rooster - Katapee
The rooster is looking for his chick.

Dog - Anton

The dog is playing with his ball.

Sheep - Colume

The sheep is leaping over the fence.

Chicken - Untoko
The chicken is going for a stroll.

Duck - Arouk
The duck is searching for the pond.

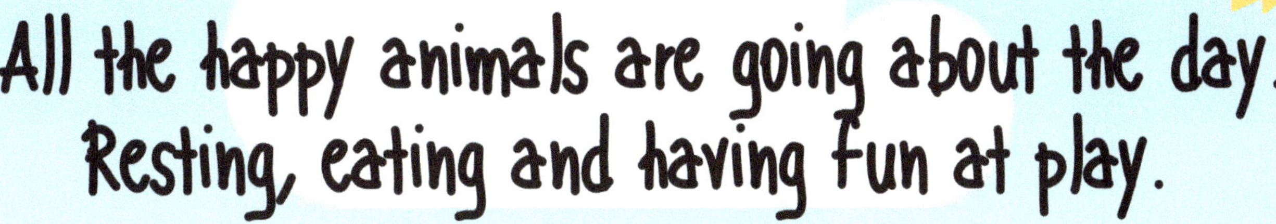
All the happy animals are going about the day.
Resting, eating and having fun at play.

Read The Animals Names

Umbook - Snake
Antikol - Snail
Ayaree - Cat
Anton - Dog
Colume - Sheep

Read The Animals Names

Untoko - Chicken

Katapee - Rooster

Kabet - Hen

Arouk - Duck

Def - Goat

Find My Temne Name

Kabet

Antikol

Umbook

Ayaree

Def

Find My Temne Name

Anton

Katapee

Colume

Arouk

Untoko

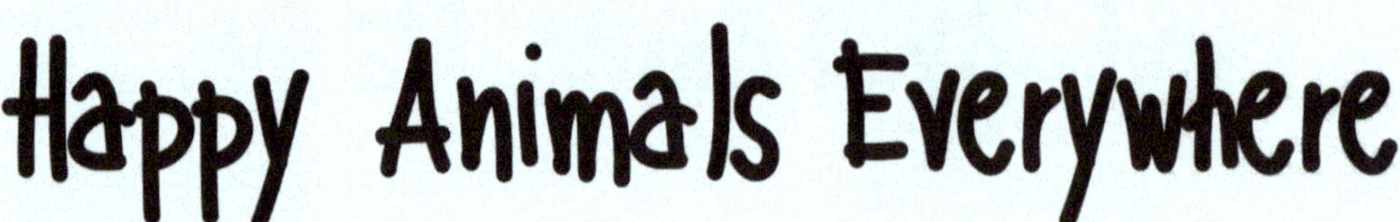
Happy Animals Everywhere

Temne Farming

The temne people are expert farmers. Rice, cassava and potato leaf are major crops farmed

Sierra Leone Rice Farming

Temne Farming

the land provides everything that we need.

Cashew nuts are healthy and nutritious. They can be used in food dishes and made into milk. They are grown in Sierra Leone and shipped worldwide.

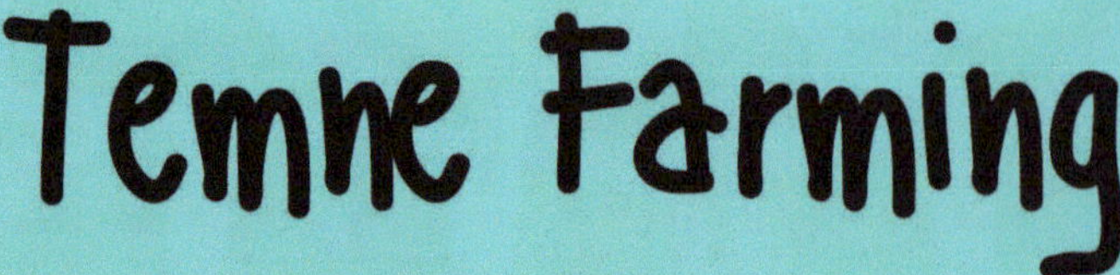

the land provides everything that we need.

Coconuts grow in Sierra Leone. they are used for many edible items including water, milk, oil and in many cooked dishes.

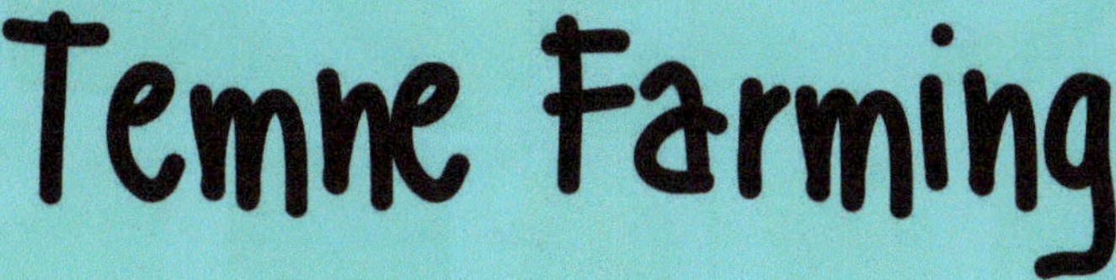

Temne Farming

the land provides everything that we need.

Mangos are a seasonal fruit. the trees are all over Sierra Leone. Mangos can be eaten fresh or used in various pureed drinks, sauces and food dishes

Temne Farming

the land provides everything that we need.

Palm tree leaves are beautiful and strong. they are used to create traditional thatch roofs, weaving baskets, palm oil, palm wine, and much more.

Sierra Leone Rice

Rice grown in Sierra Leone is a main staple food of the culture. It is served with most meals during the day. Pairing the rice with sauces, stews, various prepared meats with authentic African Spices is the traditional way.

Cassava Leaf Stew

Cassava Leaf Stew is considered to be the national dish of Sierra Leone. The dish can be prepared mild or spicy. As with most African foods, it is rich in spices and flavors. Cassava tastes great served over rice.

Potatoe Leaf Stew

Potatoe Leaf Stew is a classic dish from Sierra Leone. This dish is full of savory flavor and is served with rice or with potatoes.

About the Authors

Kendrick Simpson

Kendrick is an 8-year-old Kid Actor/Model, Author, You tuber and Entrepreneur that has an outgoing spirit and loves to teach and help others. Swimming, Basketball, Traveling and Gaming are some of his favorite things to do.

www.KidsEduCaringPlace.com
www.Kidscredible.com

About the Authors

Kenyatta Smith-Simpson

Kenyatta Smith-Simpson, M.S. Educational- Admin I is an Early Childhood Development Specialist, Preschool Education Director, Momager, Author and Wife to his amazing dad Alfred Simpson. Together we work to teach other children and families about fun, educational & cultural concepts. At KECP, instilling a love of learning is our ultimate goal.

www.KidsEduCaringPlace.com
www.Kidscredible.com

Thank You To Our Village

thank you to the temne tribe for welcoming us into the family with open arms. Returning to the motherland and visiting the village and our people has been a dream come true for us. this root strengthening journey has made a reconnection that is life changing for our family.

A Special thank You to Chief Yabomposeh, Pa Yamba & MoMoh Marrah for all of your teaching and support throughout this journey.

Happy Animals Everywhere in Temne & English

Happy Animals Everywhere in English & temne is a exploration of the language and culture of the temne People living in Sierra Leone. Many people in American have temne Tribe Ancestry. This book will help parents to teach kids to identify animals using the English words and the temne translations. Returning to the motherland and visiting the village has been a dream for us and has been life changing for our family. We are thankful to be able to share what we have learned with you.

Please shop the children's book titles in our series that teach more about various cultures and languages coming soon.
Kids Edu Caring Place -Count and Name African Animals in Swahili
Kids Edu Caring Place- Explore the temne Culture
Kids Edu Caring Place- Learn to Count In temne
and more...

KECP's Vision Publishing Statement

Kids Edu Caring Place LLC is an early learning facility in Maryland. We specialize in child development, socialization and creating optimal learning experiences for children. Our book series teaches children about a variety of fun educational concepts, history, language and culture. the goal is to help children to reconnect to that which was lost and to inspire the next generation of beautiful minds through rich cultural and educational experiences for a better future.

Dedication

Dedicated to the Ancestors.